# THE FIRST CHRISTMAS PRESENT EVER

## A Children's Program
## (In Long And Short Versions)

---

### SHERRY SANDERS

CSS Publishing Company, Inc.
Lima, Ohio

THE FIRST CHRISTMAS PRESENT EVER

Scripture quotations are from the *Revised Standard Version of the Bible,* copyrighted 1946, 1952 (c), 1971, 1973, by the Division of Christian Education of the National Council of the Churches of Christ in the USA. Used by permission.

ISBN 0-7880-0573-1                                    PRINTED IN U.S.A.

*This is dedicated to all of the children and young adults of the Sunday School Department of St. John's Lutheran Church in Meyersville. It is through the joy of directing them in St. John's annual Sunday School Christmas Eve program over the years that I gained the experience to write my book.*

# The First Christmas Present Ever
## (Long Version)

## Opening

*(A Christmas tree is in the center of the stage. Young children come in and sit on the floor around the tree. Two by two, the children come forward to the microphone to say their lines in unison. They are holding tree ornaments, and after saying their part, they hang the ornaments on the tree. The lights are already on the tree. These lines were designed for 16 children, but number could be varied by having one child say a line, two saying a line and one hanging that ornament, or group of more than two saying a line.)*

We put lights on the Christmas tree to remind us that Jesus came to be the light of the world.

Green wreaths tell us Jesus will always be with us.

The angel on the top of the tree reminds us of the angel who came to tell about Jesus.

Bells ring out the news — Jesus is born!

Candy canes make us think of the shepherds who came to see Baby Jesus.

The star shone in the sky to lead the Wise Men to Jesus.

The cross tells us why Jesus was born — to die for us!

The dove brings peace and love to everyone on earth.

*(All children come forward and sing "O Christmas Tree." When finished, they take their seats.)*

## Participants

*Non-speaking:*

| Gabriel | Lead Angel | 3 Wise Men |
|---------|-----------|-----------|
| Mary | Angels | Shepherds |
| Joseph | | |

*Speaking:*

| Grandpa | Small Child | Father |
|---------|-------------|--------|
| Mother | Older Child | 8 Readers |

Numbers of children may be varied in several ways. The Readers' parts may be shortened to accommodate more or lengthened for less students. The number of angels and shepherds is optional. The family grouping might also be altered, if necessary.

*(Group of five children come in dressed like a family: Mother, Father, Grandpa, and two children. They are carrying presents and smallest child is carrying a creche. All are placed under the tree.)*

**Small Child:** Mom, why do we put a manger scene under the Christmas tree?

**Mother:** It reminds us of the first and best Christmas present we ever received.

**Older Child:** Yea, don't you know the Christmas story? About Baby Jesus?

**Small Child:** I know it's his birthday.

**Grandpa:** Come, sit in my lap and I'll tell you about the first Christmas present.

*(Organ starts playing hymn to be sung while family settles down in corner of stage, Grandpa in rocking chair holding small child, other child on floor on pillows, Mother and Father in chairs.)*

**Congregation** sings "Oh Come, Oh Come, Emmanuel."

*(Tree and presents are removed during song. Creche is placed in view of audience. Stable or large mural of stable is set in center of stage behind family. Stable could be made from large appliance box with front cut out and some of sides cut to look like windows. Animals could be painted on back wall of stable. Manger is there also, full of hay. Readers 1 and 2 come to lectern during last verse.)*

**Grandpa:** You see, long ago a man named Joseph lived in Nazareth. And he was going to marry a woman named Mary. Now Joseph loved Mary, but even he didn't know how special Mary was. God had chosen Mary to be Jesus' mother. And one day an angel came to Mary and told her what God had said.

**Reader 1:** (Reads Luke 1:26-29)

**Reader 2:** (Reads Luke 1:30-35, 38)

*(As Reader 1 begins, Mary walks on stage away from family and stable. Angel Gabriel follows. They stand as if they are talking. When Reader 2 finishes, Gabriel leaves first, then Mary.)*

**Father:** You know, I always have to think about how Joseph must have felt — his wife having a baby that wasn't his, but who came from God.

**Mother:** I'm sure he was confused, but remember, God came to him in a dream and explained it to him. And in his own way, Joseph was a very special man, too.

**Grandpa:** That's right. Both Mary and Joseph did what God wanted them to do. But let's get back to the story.

Soon after that, Joseph had to go to Bethlehem and he took Mary with him.

**Congregation** sings "O Little Town Of Bethlehem."

**Small Child:** I know what happens then! Joseph goes to all the inns and nobody had room for them, and Mary is so tired. And that's why Jesus is born in a stable because that's the only place!

**Grandpa:** Yes, all the inns are full, and the innkeepers send them away. Except for one, who feels sorry for Mary, and he lets them stay in his stable.

*(As Grandpa starts talking, Joseph leads Mary to the stable, sets down a chair and helps her sit. He stands watching her.)*

**Small Child:** Were there animals there, Grandpa? And hay, too?

**Grandpa:** I'm sure there were. The stable was where the animals were kept and fed. But then God made something special happen — he gave us the best Christmas present ever.

**Reader 3:** (Reads Luke 2:6, 7)

*(Mary holds baby. Joseph comes and stands behind her looking at Jesus.)*

**Congregation** sings "What Child Is This?"

*(During last verse, Mary lays baby in manger and Joseph goes to other side of manger and kneels down. Reader 4 goes to lectern.)*

**Reader 4:** (Reads Luke 2:8-14)

*(As reader begins, Lead Angel comes in and stands in front facing audience, with more angels following. They remain there until after the next song.)*

**Congregation** sings "It Came Upon A Midnight Clear."

**Older Child:** So it was the angels who were the first to spread the news of Jesus' birth, right, Grandpa?

**Grandpa:** That's right. And when the shepherds were told, they didn't waste any time going to see for themselves.

*(Shepherds come from back of church, walk slowly to stable, and kneel in front of manger.)*

**Reader 5:** (Reads Luke 2:15, 16)

**Reader 6:** (Reads Luke 2:17-20)

**Grandpa:** When the shepherds left, they too went to tell the good news about Jesus.

*(Shepherds leave manger scene.)*

**Older Child:** So they were the second ones to spread the news.

**Mother:** That's right, but the message is still being spread today. Christians today are still telling the story of that first Christmas present — Jesus.

**Congregation** sings "Go Tell It On The Mountain."

**Grandpa:** But not only do we tell the story and share our joy in Jesus' birth, we also share the gifts God has blessed us with.

**Older Child:** You mean like giving our offering?

9

**Father:** Our offering, yes. But also sharing our time and talents with others for God.

**Offering**

**Congregation** sings "Joy To The World."

**Small Child:** But Grandpa, what about the star and the Wise Men? You didn't tell about them.

**Grandpa:** Well, the star was there to lead the people to Jesus — it stayed right over that stable showing the shepherds where he was, and also the Wise Men.

But the Wise Men were from a country far away. They followed the star, too, but it took them over a year of walking and riding their camels to find Jesus.

**Congregation** sings "The First Noel."

*(During third verse of song, Wise Men slowly walk from different part of church to stable. They place gifts and kneel to worship Jesus. During last verse, Readers 7 and 8 walk to lectern.)*

**Reader 7:** (Reads Matthew 2:1, 2)

**Reader 8:** (Reads Matthew 2:8-12)

**Small Child:** So the Wise Men found Jesus, too?

**Father:** That's right. God wanted all different kinds of people to know Jesus, and to receive the best Christmas present.

**Older Child:** So that's the end of the story.

**Grandpa:** Not really. The story never ends. Every year we celebrate Jesus' coming and it always seems fresh and new. And every time Jesus comes into a new believer's heart, it's like Jesus is born all over again.

**Mother:** So, Christians everywhere keep remembering and keep celebrating and keep giving thanks for the first and best Christmas present ever!

**Congregation** sings "Silent Night."

*(As organ plays through verse, all angels, shepherds, Wise Men, readers stand around manger scene with Mary, Joseph and Baby Jesus, as all sing. Spotlight on Mary, Joseph and baby.)*

# The First Christmas Present Ever
## (Short Version)

**Opening**

*(Young children stand in rows holding ornaments appropriate to lines they will say. Number of children may be varied by one, two, or more children saying lines in unison.)*

We put lights on the Christmas tree to remind us that Jesus came to be the light of the world.

Green wreaths tell us Jesus will always be with us.

The angel on the top of the tree reminds us of the angel who came to tell about Jesus.

Bells ring out the news — Jesus is born!

Candy canes make us think of the shepherds who came to see Baby Jesus.

The star shone in the sky to lead the Wise Men to Jesus.

The cross tells us why Jesus was born — to die for us!

The dove brings peace and love to everyone on earth.

*(When all have spoken, they take their seats.)*

**Participants**

*Non-speaking:*

| | | |
|---|---|---|
| Gabriel | Lead Angel | 3 Wise Men |
| Mary | Angels | Shepherds |
| Joseph | | |

*Speaking:*

| | | |
|---|---|---|
| Grandpa | Small Child | Father |
| Mother | Older Child | 8 Readers |

Numbers of children may be varied in several ways. The Readers' parts may be shortened to accommodate more or lengthened for less students. The number of angels and shepherds is optional. The family grouping might also be altered, if necessary.

*(Group of five children come in dressed like a family: Mother, Father, Grandpa, and two children. Smallest child is carrying a creche.)*

**Small Child:** Mom, why do we put the manger scene up at Christmas?

**Mother:** It reminds us of the first and best Christmas present we ever received.

**Older Child:** Yea, don't you know the Christmas story? About Baby Jesus?

**Small Child:** I know it's his birthday.

**Grandpa:** Come, sit in my lap and I'll tell you about the first Christmas present.

*(Family settles down in corner of stage: Grandpa in rocking chair holding small child, other child on floor on pillows, Mother and Father in chairs. Creche is placed in view of audience. Stable or large mural of stable is set in center of stage*

14

*behind family. Stable could be made from large appliance box with front cut out and some of sides cut to look like windows. Animals could be painted on back wall of stable. Manger is also there, full of hay. Readers 1 and 2 come to lectern.)*

**Grandpa:** You see, long ago a man named Joseph lived in Nazareth. And he was going to marry a woman named Mary. Now Joseph loved Mary, but even he didn't know how special Mary was. God had chosen Mary to be Jesus' mother. And one day an angel came to Mary and told her what God had said.

**Reader 1:** (Reads Luke 1:26-29)

**Reader 2:** (Reads Luke 1:30-35, 38)

*(As Reader 1 begins, Mary walks on stage away from family and stable. Angel Gabriel follows. They stand as if they are talking. When Reader 2 finishes, Gabriel leaves first, then Mary.)*

**Father:** You know, I always have to think about how Joseph must have felt — his wife having a baby that wasn't his, but who came from God.

**Mother:** I'm sure he was confused, but remember, God came to him in a dream and explained it to him. And in his own way, Joseph was a very special man, too.

**Grandpa:** That's right. Both Mary and Joseph did what God wanted them to do. But let's get back to the story.
 Soon after that, Joseph had to go to Bethlehem and he took Mary with him.

**Small Child:** I know what happens then! Joseph goes to all the inns and nobody has room for them, and Mary is so tired. And that's why Jesus is born in a stable because that's the only place!

**Grandpa:** Yes, all the inns are full, and the innkeepers send them away. Except for one, who feels sorry for Mary, and he lets them stay in his stable.

*(As Grandpa starts talking, Joseph leads Mary to the stable, sets down a chair and helps her sit. He stands watching her.)*

**Small Child:** Were there animals there, Grandpa? And hay, too?

**Grandpa:** I'm sure there were. The stable was where the animals were kept and fed. But then God made something special happen — he gave us the best Christmas present ever.

**Reader 3:** (Reads Luke 2:6, 7)

*(Mary holds baby. Joseph comes and stands behind her looking at Jesus. Mary lays baby in manger and Joseph goes to other side of manger and kneels down. Reader 4 goes to lectern.)*

**Reader 4:** (Reads Luke 2:8-14)

*(As reader begins, Lead Angel comes in and stands in front facing audience, with more angels following. They remain there until Older Child begins talking.)*

**Older Child:** So it was the angels who were the first to spread the news of Jesus' birth, right, Grandpa?

**Grandpa:** That's right. And when the shepherds were told, they didn't waste any time going to see for themselves.

*(Shepherds come from back of church, walk slowly to stable, and kneel in front of manger.)*

**Reader 5:** (Reads Luke 2:15, 16)

**Reader 6:** (Reads Luke 2:17-20)

**Grandpa:** When the shepherds left, they too went to tell the good news about Jesus.

*(Shepherds leave manger scene.)*

**Older Child:** So they were the second ones to spread the news.

**Mother:** That's right, but the message is still being spread today. Christians today are still telling the story of that first Christmas present — Jesus.

**Grandpa:** But not only do we tell the story and share our joy in Jesus' birth, we also share the gifts God has blessed us with.

**Older Child:** You mean like giving our offering?

**Father:** Our offering, yes. But also sharing our time and talents with others for God.

**Small Child:** But Grandpa, what about the star and the Wise Men? You didn't tell about them.

**Grandpa:** Well, the star was there to lead the people to Jesus — it stayed right over that stable showing the shepherds where he was, and also the Wise Men.
But the Wise Men were from a country far away. They followed the star, too, but it took them over a year of walking and riding their camels to find Jesus.

**Reader 7:** (Reads Matthew 2:1, 2)

**Reader 8:** (Reads Matthew 2:8-12)

*(As readers begin, Wise Men enter from different part of church and walk to stable. They place gifts and kneel down to worship Jesus.)*

17

**Small Child:** So the Wise Men found Jesus, too?

**Father:** That's right. God wanted all different kinds of people to know Jesus, and to receive the best Christmas present.

**Older Child:** So that's the end of the story.

**Grandpa:** Not really. The story never ends. Every year we celebrate Jesus' coming and it always seems fresh and new. And every time Jesus comes into a new believer's heart, it's like Jesus is born all over again.

**Mother:** So, Christians everywhere keep remembering and keep celebrating and keep giving thanks for the first and best Christmas present ever!